A FRIEND IN THE LIBRARY

NATURE

BY

EVA MARCH TAPPAN

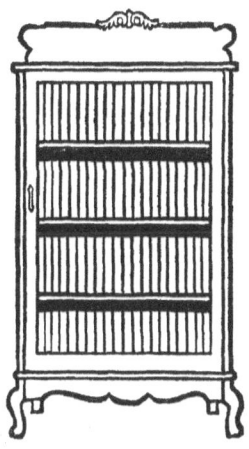

British Library Cataloguing-in-Publication Data
A catalogue record for this book is available from the
British Library

NATURE

A FRIEND IN THE LIBRARY

A Practical Guide to the Writings of

RALPH WALDO EMERSON

NATHANIEL HAWTHORNE

HENRY WADSWORTH LONGFELLOW

JAMES RUSSELL LOWELL

JOHN GREENLEAF WHITTIER

OLIVER WENDELL HOLMES

IN TWELVE VOLUMES

VOLUME IX

Eva March Tappan

Eva March Tappan was born on 26th December 1854 in Blackstone, Massachusetts, America. She is well known as a factual as well as fictional writer, but spent her early career as a teacher. Tappan was the only child of Reverend Edmund March Tappan and Lucretia Logée, and received her education at the esteemed Vassar College. This was a private coeducational liberal arts college, in the town of Poughkeepsie, New York, from which she graduated in 1875. Here, Tappan was a member of Phi Beta Kappa, the oldest honour society for the liberal arts and sciences, widely considered as the nations most prestigious society. She also edited the *Vassar Miscellany,* a college publication.

After leaving her early education, Tappan began teaching at Wheaton College, one of the oldest institutions of higher education for women in the United States, founded in 1834 and based in Norton, Massachusetts. She taught Latin and German here, from 1875 until 1880, before moving on to the Raymond Academy in Camden, New Jersey where she was associate Principal until 1894. Tappan also received a graduate degree in English Literature from the University of Pennsylvania. This allowed her to pursue her first love, that of reading and writing, and she taught as head of the English department at the English High School at Worcester, Massachusetts.

It was only after this date that Tappan began her literary career, writing about famous characters in history, often aimed at educating children in important historical themes and epochs. Some of her better known works include, *In the Days of William the Conqueror* (1901) and *In the Days of Queen Elizabeth* (1902), *The Out-of-Door Book* (1907), *When Knights Were Bold* (1911) and *The Little Book of the Flag* (1917). Tappan never married, being a happy singleton, and died on 29th January 1930, aged seventy-five.

NATURE

SEVERAL years ago a lady and a few young folk, in a tiny village by the sea, met as teacher and pupils. The teacher liked to be out of doors, and the pupils were ready to like whatever she liked. As soon as lesson hours were over, the whole little company started for the boat, or the carriage, or a long tramp through the woods or on the shore. The teacher was not trying to teach, and the boys and girls were not trying to learn; they were simply enjoying themselves; but years afterwards one of the young people said, "As time goes on, I realize more and more how much I am indebted to her for opening my eyes to see beauty in nature."

There is always plenty of beauty to see, if there is only some one with eyes to see it. Lowell says ("A Good Word for Winter," i. 337) that "eyes are not so common as people think"; and Emerson declares ("Nature," iii. 176), "The difference between landscape and landscape is small, but there is great difference in the beholders." There is a story of an artist who painted a shed door not only with the gray of the weather-beaten wood, but with all the play of vague and flitting colors which he saw when the sun shone upon it. Some one glanced at the picture and said scornfully, "I never saw a shed door look like that." The artist quietly retorted, "Don't you wish you could?" It is worth a great deal to know how to see.

The poet knows how to see, or else he could

not be a poet. He can see beauty, not only in the wonderful circlings of the planets and the glories of the sunsets, but in the little things that so often slip past us unnoticed. He marks the ripples on the sand beach, the swing of the tide, the driving of a cloud, the unfolding of a flower, the "loud and sudden rush of wings" when a flock of birds rises into the air. There is often beauty so common that we have forgotten to note it. We see that rocks are gray, but not every one has noticed that in the early morning, at the rising of the sun, an exquisite rosy glow comes upon them. Whittier has noted this, and it is good to have him call our attention to it. He writes ("A Sea Dream," ii. 67) of

> Two gray rocks touched with tender bloom
> Beneath the fresh-blown rose of dawn.

Lowell writes of the coloring of the snow ("A Good Word for Winter," i. 337) : —

I have spoken of the exquisite curves of snow surfaces. Not less rare are the tints of which they are capable, — the faint blue of the hollows, for the shadows in snow are always blue, and the tender rose of higher points, as you stand with your back to the setting sun and look upward across the soft rondure of a hillside. I have seen, within a mile of home, effects of color as lovely as any iridescence of the Silberhorn after sundown.

The poet can not only see for himself, he can make us see. He can paint a picture for us. He can show us that the common things around us are so beautiful that we shall wonder we have never thought of their beauty before. Painting a picture is entirely different from giving a matter-of-fact description. The botanist's description of a dandelion, for instance, is accurate and definite, but it gives us no idea of beauty and it paints no picture. The botanist says: "Head many-flowered, large, solitary, on a slender hollow scape. Involucre double, the outer of short scales; the inner of long linear scales;" and so it goes on through many lines of fine print. The description is useful, but I do not believe that any one ever loved a dandelion the better for reading it, or that it ever made any one happier or gave him a pleasant thought. Once the poet Lowell wrote of a dandelion ("To the Dandelion," ix. 230), and this is what he said:—

Dear common flower, that grow'st beside the way,
Fringing the dusty road with harmless gold.

No one could read those two lines without a happy little smile of remembrance. He calls to mind some "dusty road" with its fringe of golden blossoms. A gleam of the poet's own tenderness has shone into his heart, and when he sees the dandelion again, he is likely to say to himself, "Dear common flower."

Here is another picture, painted by Whittier, of the morning after a heavy snowfall. It is from "Snow-Bound" (ii. 134); and the whole poem is, indeed, a vivid portrayal of country life as he knew it when a boy.

> Next morn we wakened with the shout
> Of merry voices high and clear;
> And saw the teamsters drawing near
> To break the drifted highways out.
> Down the long hillside treading slow
> We saw the half-buried oxen go,
> Shaking the snow from heads uptost,
> Their straining nostrils white with frost.
> Before our door the straggling train
> Drew up, an added team to gain.

6

NATURE

The elders threshed their hands a-cold,
  Passed, with the cider-mug, their jokes
  From lip to lip; the younger folks
Down the loose snow-banks, wrestling, rolled;
Then toiled again the cavalcade
  O'er windy hill, through clogged ravine,
  And woodland paths that wound between
Low drooping pine-boughs winter-weighed.

Whittier makes no attempt at "fine writing":
he paints a simple winter scene in the coun-
try; but he chooses just the objects that bring
it before us and that show the homelikeness
of it. Maybe, if we had seen it ourselves, we
should not have recognized that it was a pic-
ture; but now that the poet has shown it to us,
it is our own. We are the richer for having it
in our memories, and, moreover, we are more
ready to recognize other pictures where we
might perhaps have thought there were none.

7

The poet can not only paint a picture, but he can interpret its meaning. At the opening of "Evangeline" (ii. 19), Longfellow says: —

This is the forest primeval. The murmuring pines and
the hemlocks,
Bearded with moss, and in garments green, indistinct
in the twilight,
Stand like Druids of eld, with voices sad and prophetic,
Stand like harpers hoar, with beards that rest on their
bosoms.

Here is the picture and also the poet's interpretation. The pines and hemlocks are tall and dignified and mysterious and sad. If he had described them as being gay and merry and jubilant, the lines would have been forgotten long ago; but we feel instinctively that his interpretation is the true one, and that is why thousands of people have repeated them on entering a forest of pines and hemlocks.

Another way in which the poet can interpret is by using just the right phrase. Our language is full of poetical phrases, and they are so common that we sometimes forget they are poetry; but the real poet is sure to find occasion for some new phrase that will express his thought better than any that has been used before. In describing the Friends' meeting, where many gather together and often sit in reverent stillness, Whittier speaks ("The Meeting," ii. 278) of

> The silence multiplied
> By these still forms on either side.

Silence cannot be more still than silence; and yet the phrase "silence multiplied" does make it seem as if in that Friends' meeting it was more still than stillness itself. Lowell calls the birch "most shy and ladylike of trees" ("An Indian-Summer Reverie," ix. 193); and the thought slips into one's mind whenever he sees the coy white birch, slender and graceful, half leaning toward the narrow road and half drawing back from it.

To see and to interpret are the gift of the poet, but he can do even more than these, for to nature and her meaning he can add some thought of his own which the object suggests to him, so strong or wise or beautiful that it would hardly have come to any one except a poet. Longfellow's poems are full of these thoughts. For instance, he says of the simple Acadian farmers ("Evangeline," ii. 19):—

Men whose lives glided on like rivers that water the woodlands,
Darkened by shadows of earth, but reflecting an image of heaven.

NATURE

Of the fair maiden Evangeline he says:—

When she had passed, it seemed like the ceasing of
exquisite music.

The lighthouse, far out on the point of the
rocky ledge, reminds him of the giant who
used his mighty strength to help pilgrims over
the flood, and he says ("The Lighthouse," i.
298):—

Like the great giant Christopher it stands
  Upon the brink of the tempestuous wave,
Wading far out among the rocks and sands,
  The night-o'ertaken mariner to save.

He sees the waves break on the distant ledge,
so far away that they cannot be heard, and he
calls them

A speechless wrath, that rises and subsides
  In the white lip and tremor of the face.

11

The compass brings to his mind the thought
("The Building of the Ship," i. 277): —

> Ah! if our souls but poise and swing
> Like the compass in its brazen ring,
> Ever level and ever true
> To the toil and the task we have to do,
> We shall sail securely and safely reach
> The Fortunate Isles, on whose shining beach
> The sights we see, and the sounds we hear,
> Will be those of joy and not of fear!

It is a common enough sight to see a little brook trickling down a stony hillside; but when Longfellow looks upon it, it suggests a little child, venturing timidly down a stair, and he writes ("Mad River," iii. 323): —

> A brooklet nameless and unknown
>   Was I at first, resembling
> A little child, that all alone
> Comes venturing down the stairs of stone,
>   Irresolute and trembling.

More than once Longfellow speaks of the wind as a strong man. In "The Lighthouse" (i. 298) he says that against the house

Press the great shoulders of the hurricane.

In another poem ("Daybreak," iii. 56) he says: —

A wind came up out of the sea,
And said, "O mists, make room for me."

Longfellow gives the thought that the wind arouses in him, that it is as a strong man prepared to run a race and thrusting the mists from his path. Emerson's "The Snow-Storm" (ix. 41) is a most excellent picture of a storm; but it is more, for the poet adds to it the fancy that the north wind is alive and has made a merry night of it with his "frolic architecture." Here Emerson tells us not only what he sees, but what he thinks and feels and fancies. He permits us to know his thoughts and to think with him.

To see as the poet sees and to think with him is a glorious privilege; but there is one thing even better, for a poet often has power to express something that we have half felt, but have never been able to put into words. Whittier says ("A Mystery," ii. 66): —

> The secret which the mountains kept,
> The river never told.

Emerson writes ("The World-Soul," ix. 15):

> Stars taunt us by a mystery
> Which we could never spell.

Every one who gazes at the mountains and the stars feels vaguely that in them there is something beyond us, something that we cannot read; and the poets have put the thought into words. So it is with many other things. We

know, if we stop to think, that the song of the
wild bird would not be so sweet within walls,
that shells and mosses are not so beautiful in
a house as on the seashore. Emerson feels
this also, and he says ("Each and All," ix.
4): —

I thought the sparrow's note from heaven,
Singing at dawn on the alder bough;
I brought him home in his nest, at even;
He sings the song, but it cheers not now,
For I did not bring home the river and sky; —
He sang to my ear, — they sang to my eye.
The delicate shells lay on the shore;
The bubbles of the latest wave
Fresh pearls to their enamel gave,
And the bellowing of the savage sea
Greeted their safe escape to me.
I wiped away the weeds and foam,
I fetched my sea-born treasures home;
But the poor, unsightly, noisome things

Had left their beauty on the shore
With the sun and the sand and the wild uproar.

Perhaps we have not found out why the beauty has vanished, but the poet can tell us why, and he explains: —

All are needed by each one;
Nothing is fair or good alone.

The poet has the gift of expression, and he can put into words what others only feel. He gives us a share in his genius, and rightfully, for no poem would live unless there was something in us that responded to it, something that whispered, "That is true."

Now, on a country walk one may get a great deal of pleasure from seeing the flowers that grow in the sunlight and in open view; but sometimes it is a delight to search for them, to push away the dry leaves, and find the pink beauty and sweetness of the trailing arbutus. So it is with the poems on nature. There is much to be enjoyed even at a glance; but there is also a pleasure in looking a little closer, in reading slowly and thinking between the lines. In every real poem there is much more to be found than appears on the surface. Take Emerson's "The Humble Bee" (ix. 38), for instance. First read it through aloud. Notice whether any of the lines are especially smooth or especially difficult to read rhythmically. Then turn back to the first stanza. Stop a moment to think why Emerson calls the humble-bee "burly." Why should he call it "dozing"? Is it because the bee itself is sleepy, or because it makes a drowsy, sleepy noise? Why should the bee suggest a hot climate? Which phrase expresses this with most originality? Why call the bee "a lover of the sun"? Why call it "Epicurean of June"? What is the meaning of the last line of the second stanza? In the third stanza, just what is meant by "Silvers the horizon wall"? The line, "Turns the sod to violets," calls to mind an expression in Lowell's description of a June day in "The Vision of Sir Launfal" (ix. 301); which is it? Why is this an especially poetical line? Why should Emerson call the silence "green"? Why talk of *Indian* wildernesses and *Syrian* peace? Why should leisure be called "immortal"? Which is the most poetical line in the fifth stanza? What does the last line mean? What two lines in the closing stanza give the moral of the poem? Is it true? Would it be a good working motto for people as well as bees? What words in the poem show that the poet noticed color, light, sound, motion, fragrance? If this poem were to be illustrated, which lines would make the best pictures? Why would not the metre of Longfellow's "Evangeline" (ii. 19) be suitable for this poem? Is it truthful in its descriptions, that is, does a bee make "waving lines"? When the south wind blows, does it "Silver the horizon wall"? Does succory "match the sky"? Is fern "scented"?

"The Vision of Sir Launfal" (Lowell, ix. 299) is a fine poem to study in this way. Read the brief introduction about the beautiful legend that is its foundation. Read the whole poem through, and then begin to think about it. What relation is there between the Preludes and the main body of the poem? Why does the poet write about June in the First

Prelude and about December in the Second? If only two lines in the First Prelude could be saved, which would be best worth keeping? In the stanza beginning, "And what is so rare as a day in June?" which expressions simply state facts, and which express them in forms that would not be found in ordinary prose? Prove that Lowell noticed closely. Why should this picture of a June day be so famous? By what reasoning does he come to the last two lines of the First Prelude? In Part First, why should Sir Launfal call for his richest armor? In the second stanza, what are some of the poetical expressions? What fine contrast is pictured? What is meant by "pavilions tall" and "Green and broad was every tent"? How could the third stanza be illustrated? In the fifth stanza what is the meaning of "made morn"? Why is the leper drawn as so loathsome? What comparison is in the stanza and why is it good? Is the speech of the leper true? What is the meaning of the fifth line? Did Sir Launfal give purely "from a sense of duty"?

In the Prelude to Part Second, what poetical similes are there? Which lines show most clearly that Lowell kept his eyes open to the beauties of nature? How does it increase the interest of the first stanza to speak of the brook as if it were a person? (See Lowell, xiv. 200, to find where this brook is.) Compare the last six lines of the first stanza with the closing lines of Emerson's "The Snow-Storm" (ix. 41). Which do you prefer, and why? Compare the closing lines of the second stanza : —

And swift little troops of silent sparks,
    Now pausing, now scattering away as in fear,
Go threading the soot-forest's tangled darks
    Like herds of startled deer,

with Longfellow's simile in "Evangeline" (ii.
27) where the children

Oft on autumnal eves, when without in the gathering
    darkness
Bursting with light seemed the smithy, through every
    cranny and crevice,
Warm by the forge within they watched the laboring
    bellows,
And as its panting ceased, and the sparks expired in
    the ashes,
Merrily laughed, and said they were nuns going into
    the chapel.

Why would not Longfellow's simile be appropriate in "Sir Launfal"? In the last stanza of the Second Prelude how does Lowell show that many years have passed? In Part Second compare the details of the second stanza with those of the second stanza in Part First. Why should Sir Launfal muse of the desert? In the sixth stanza, what is the meaning of the last two lines? A group of six lines in Part Second is famous; which best deserve fame? Notice how perfectly Lowell makes nature sympathize with the story. Notice that the poem shows an accurate knowledge of nature, but puts that knowledge in exquisitely poetical form. Notice, too, that the poem is not only a story of a knight searching for the Holy Grail, but an allegory of a human life.

After studying about poems, study separate authors. All may see the same objects of nature, but no two treat them in quite the same way. Whittier writes of nature, as in "The Barefoot Boy" (ii. 126), with a country boy's accurate knowledge of what he himself has seen. Lowell has seen as accurately, perhaps even more minutely, but he describes with a scholar's richness of phrase and association. Longfellow loves to add a simile. Everything in nature seems to him like something in human life. To Emerson, nature is the expression of a thought of God. He loves the rose, but he also reverences it because it has a message from God to men. Holmes can hardly help a bit of jesting. He treats "the last leaf upon the tree" ("The Last Leaf," xii. 3) with whimsical pathos; the "September Gale" (xii. 29) with mock regret; against the katydid he brings the weighty charge ("To an Insect," xii. 9), —

> Thou say'st an undisputed thing
> In such a solemn way.

But when Holmes consents to lay aside his merry wit for a moment, he produces such a masterpiece as "The Chambered Nautilus" (xii. 393), one of the noblest poems ever written of nature and of life. With Hawthorne, an object of nature points the way to a parable. A face of rock on a mountain-side suggests the story of "The Great Stone Face" (iii. 29). Even the rooster and the hen in "The House of the Seven Gables" (vii.) are forlorn parodies, comical and pathetic under-studies of Clifford and Hepzibah.

So it is that the poet can see and can interpret nature for us, can give us thoughts of his own, can express what we have only half felt; but is it worth while? A rather stolid farmer once gazed at his wife's flower-bed and walked away, shaking his head and saying, "Very pretty, very pretty, but they're neither potatoes nor corn." We all need the "potatoes and corn," but does it take anything from the value of the potato to realize that it has a pretty flower? Does not a field of corn grow just as well if it suggests to its owner Whittier's "Corn-Song" (iii. 312)?

> All through the long, bright days of June,
> Its leaves grew green and fair,
> And waved in hot midsummer's noon
> Its soft and yellow hair.

Emerson says in one of his essays on Nature (iii. 172): —

It seems as if the day was not wholly profane in which we have given heed to some natural object. The fall of snowflakes in a still air, preserving to each crystal its perfect form; the blowing of sleet over a wide field of water, and over plains; the waving rye-fields; the mimic waving of acres of houstonia, whose innumerable florets whiten and ripple before the eye; the reflections of trees and flowers in glassy lakes; the musical, steaming, odorous south wind, which converts all trees to wind-harps; the crackling and spurting of hemlock in the flames, or of pine logs, which yield glory to the walls and faces in the sitting-room, — these are the music and pictures of the most ancient religion.

But reading takes time, and we are the busiest of people. Is not poetry one of the luxuries that must be set aside for those who have wealth and "immortal leisure"? I think not. Lincoln gained his first knowledge of law by writing one paragraph of a law book at a time on a bit of shingle, when he was going to the field, by thinking about it while he worked, and reading it whenever he stopped a minute to rest; and I am not sure but this would be an ideal way to learn poetry. A poem on nature is almost always full of pleasant thoughts, thoughts that are good to have in mind to smooth out some of the lines from the care-worn face and lessen some of the troubles of the anxious heart. To know the poetry of the woods and the fields, the ocean and the mountains, gives a richness and fullness to life that nothing else can afford. Matthew Arnold declares that "More and more mankind will discover that we have to turn to poetry to interpret life for us, to console, to sustain us." He who knows even one good poem is never friendless, is never entirely alone.

NATURE

ADDITIONAL

Emerson

Country Life, xii. 133.
The Rhodora, ix. 37.
Woodnotes, ix. 43.
Monadnoc, ix. 60.
May-Day, ix. 163.
My Garden, ix. 229.
The Titmouse, ix. 233.
April, ix. 255.
Forbearance, ix. 83.
Concord Walks, xii. 169.
Farming, vii. 135.

Lowell

My Garden Acquaintance, i. 259.
A Moosehead Journal, i. 71.
A Summer Storm, ix. 20.
Midnight, ix. 44.
To a Pine-Tree, ix. 173.
Beaver Brook, ix. 278.
Under the Willows, iv. 152.
Al Fresco, iv. 178.

Pictures from Appledore, iv. 201.
Biglow Papers, No. III., xi. 209–212.

HOLMES

Lines recited at the Berkshire Jubilee, xii. 82.
The Living Temple, xii. 252.
Spring Has Come, xii. 401.
My Aviary, xiii. 214.
The Secret of the Stars, xiii. 378.

HAWTHORNE

Buds and Bird Voices, iv. 205.
The Old Manse, iv. 1.

LONGFELLOW

Flowers, i. 26.
Autumn, i. 38.
The Spirit of Poetry, i. 45.
Rain in Summer, i. 227.
The Occultation of Orion, i. 237.
Afternoon in February, i. 248.
Seaweed, i. 290.
The Secret of the Sea, i. 293.

NATURE

WHITTIER

QUESTIONS

1. What is the difference between a botanist's description of a flower and a poet's?
   The botanist's is accurate ; the poet's paints a picture or notes a simile.

2. What is the poet's noblest work in his nature poems?
   To interpret.

3. Find three similes in "Evangeline" (ii. 17).

4. Name one of Longfellow's poems of labor.
   "The Building of the Ship" (i. 277).

5. Where may the best description of a June day be found?
   In "The Vision of Sir Launfal" (ix. 299).

6. How does Whittier write of nature?
   With a country boy's accurate knowledge of what he has seen.

7. How does Lowell?

    With both accuracy and a scholar's richness of phrase and association.

8. How does Longfellow?

    He is especially fond of adding a simile.

9. How does Emerson?

    He looks upon nature as the expression of a thought of God.

10. How does Holmes?

    He enjoys a bit of jesting, but is capable of a most noble treatment of nature subjects.

11. How does Hawthorne?

    He always sees a parable in nature.

12. Why is it worth while to read poems on nature?

    Because they fill the mind with pleasant thoughts.

13. What poem pictures Whittier's boyhood?

    "The Barefoot Boy" (ii. 126).

33

14. Which poem pictures the boyhood of Long-fellow?

   "My Lost Youth" (iii. 39).

15. Name three good descriptive poems on winter.

   The Prelude to Part Second in "The Vision of Sir Launfal" (i. 299); *Emerson's "The Snow-Storm"* (ix. 41); *and Whittier's "Snow-Bound"* (ii. 134).

16. Why do poems on familiar subjects like "To the Dandelion" (ix. 230) please us?

   Because they call to mind familiar scenes and point out beauty where we may not have noticed it before.

17. Why is a simile like the one quoted in the lines from Longfellow's "Mad River" (iii. 323) pleasing?

   Because it brings a beautiful picture to the mind, and thus enriches the poem as an illustration enriches a book.

18. Name a poem that expresses what many feel, but cannot put into words.

    "Each and All" (*Emerson,* ix. 4).

19. Why is it of value to study a poem?

    Because by so doing one may discover many beauties besides those that lie on the surface.

20. In Longfellow's "Evangeline" (ii. 32–33), find six poetical expressions.

21. Select all the poetical expressions in Emerson's "The Humble-Bee" (ix. 38).